Presentation by *BookLeaf Publishing*

Web: www.bookleafpub.com

E-mail: info@bookleafpub.com

ISBN: 9789358315097
First edition 2024

midlife toasts and tongue-twisters

Jay New

BookLeaf
Publishing

India | USA | UK

For all my niblings, including Emari.

ACKNOWLEDGEMENT

Thanks to Fiona, James, Sarah, Bethany, Anderson, Nora, Mike, Lake, and especially Sharonda for providing the motivation. Your magic words inspire me.

PREFACE

My sister is the poet of the family; I didn't think I was a poet. I, too, majored in English, but just never got into poetry.

I used to blame it on the eccentric professor who taught my Intro to Poetry class in college. Rather than using conventional methods for introducing poetry, he chose to teach us his life's work: an elaborate, systematic process for analyzing any poem. Imagine a balding guy with dark pants and a dark turtleneck with pancake-sized smudges of white on his knees from gleefully tapping out rhythms with chalk-caked hands. His system was intriguing, but not particularly good for teaching me to appreciate poems.

Nearly everything about me has changed over the past five-ish years, including my writing. After all the topsy-turvy, poetry just makes so much more sense. It feels like I'm learning from the inside out, rather than outside in.

to childhood!

running around and around the house
how fast can I go?

going round and round the world
so much so
that I thought someday
I would go to the moon

and not only that–
I would know
how to fly the spaceship
scenic route to go
all the way out to the farthest reaches of our
universe and back
hoping I would get to know

life's treasures beyond every horizon
I'd ever known
before

to childhood!

to pets!

pets are people too
no matter what you say
I have so many examples
to share with you today

let's start with Mr. Goldfish
whom I met at the arcade
he joined me in my classroom
and he got a better grade!

next I'll mention Sweetheart
our darling cockatiel
she's popular and gorgeous
and she always keeps it real

I can't forget Mathilda
with their giant tortoise shell
they have a lot of baggage
and they carry it so well

if you don't know Mathilda,
Mr. Goldfish or Sweetheart
I hope you know some animals
and cultivate the art

of making friends with animals
like those who always knew
that people are all animals
and pets are people too

to siblings and niblings!

big ones, little ones, middle ones too
whether live-in friends or estranged

the bigs have so many things to do
and they don't want their stuff rearranged
the littles dance around the room
attracting visitors' mention
the middles don't mean to be acting out
they're just seeking a little attention

they're the leader of the pack
she breaks all the rules
you want to get your teddy back?
sibling! he's playing with your tools!

see, we get along quite well sometimes
(when we're not acting like fools)

we are alone and not alone
together and apart
wherever the "wind" blows you
I'll hold you in my heart…

oh and that reminds me:
please go outside to fart - thanks!

to siblings and niblings!

to cousins!

we get to see our cousins!
the allure of vacations from school
we'll brag about our social scene
just so they'll know we're cool

games and sports and eating
also swimming in the pool
golf clubs, gloves and baseballs
maybe a diving board too

what outfit will impress them?
what poster for my room?
we don't see cousins everyday
and we get to see them soon!

we'll try to put on bathing suits
too skimpy for our mothers
we'll tiptoe through the rooms
and draw mustaches on our brothers

we'll see how we're alike
family members to each other
we'll also see how different
we can be from one another

a very special mention
goes to all my older ones
who took me to the movies
counseled camp
and shot squirt guns

to cousins!

teatime sing-along

(to the tune of "She'll be Comin' Round the Mountain")

Sibling Grey is on their way to make some tea
Sibling Grey is on their way to make some tea
They said they are on their way to make tea for
us today!
Sibling Grey is on their way to make some tea

They're preparing herbs and tinctures for the tea
They're preparing herbs and tinctures for the tea
Herbs and tinctures for the tea - they are tasty
and dairy-free
They're preparing herbs and tinctures for the tea

They are setting up a table for the tea
They are setting up a table for the tea
With a table for the tea, they can sit with you
and me
They are setting up a table for the tea

Sibling Grey is almost ready to serve tea
Sibling Grey is almost ready to serve tea
When they ring the bell times three, tea is ready,
come and see!

Now it's time to welcome guests for the tea

Brother Lonely is on his way to tea
Brother Lonely is on his way to tea
Brother Lonely doesn't know which way to go
I said he could come along with me

Sister Dirty is on her way to tea
Sister Dirty's on her merry way to tea
She stumbled on her path, now she wants to take
a bath
I said come on in, the bathtub will be free

Cousin Bigshot is on their way to tea
Cousin Bigshot is on their way to tea
It seems they can't really see past their own two
feet
They're expecting fancy service at the tea

Sister Meek is on her way to tea
She is coming to chat with you and me
She's so humble, so unique - we should listen
when she speaks
I'm so glad that Sister Meek will come to tea

Mother Dear is on her way to tea
Mother Dear is on her way for tea with me
When she's tickled as can be, don't make her
laugh - there will be pee

She'll be laughing at your jokes over tea

We welcome our friends to come for tea
Our friends are like family
If you don't drink tea, we'll make coffee - don't
worry
Please come over to my house for some tea

Sibling Grey, thanks for hosting a tea party
Now, do you want us to make you some tea?
To be honest, that would be exactly what I need
Pour me some of that magic potion we call tea

ground, ground, ground yourself

(to the tune of "Row, Row, Row Your Boat")

ground, ground, ground yourself
in your own body
slowly, gently coming down
to the earth with me

ground, ground, ground yourself
with something sensory
notice 3 things you hear, 2 you smell
and 1 that you can see

ground yourself and take a breath
very mindfully
in on 1, hold on 2
breathe out and count to 3

ground, ground, ground yourself
for you it looks easy
when I can't get myself out of bed
impossible it seems

another way to ground yourself
if you're panicking

a frozen ice pack to your chest
or a bag of frozen peas

ground, ground, ground yourself
in your own body
slowly, gently coming down
to the earth with me

lessons in childhood in lessons

they say, say they
sticks and stones and stones and sticks
may they break any bones, bones any break they
may

if you say words never hurt, never words say
you if

confused my literal brain is, brain literal my
confused
when did words stop being violent? violent
being stop words did when?

kids are mean—so mean sometimes, brutal!
sometimes mean, so mean are kids
true, very true

mostly aiming for buttons, pushing buttons for
aiming mostly
us blaming each other, each blaming us
teasing connects sometimes - only sometimes
connects teasing

they do trample timidity, trample do they

real pain makes disconnect, makes pain real
do we try to connect to us? to connect to try we
do
we want, need, must connect! connect must need
want we

aware be aware be aware be aware
we protect us protect we

intro to geometry poetry

15

what   is   poetry   ?

is   it   living   ?

my   brain   painting   ?

poetry   power   moving ?

?   ?   ?
?

                   circles can
            provide   curve
        when
you
      want
curve
      circles
give
      balance
        if
   that
is

what   you
really
        need
so
               don't
worry

          when   mere
          circles   surround
             you're safe and sound

alternating   shapes   of   words

sounds   thoughts   emotions

taking   on   poetically

geometric   character

or   form

<3

no grammatical us

grey dog <3 big :)

cat orange snuggle lazy

human friend away today

smile laugh play pet

lucky.

get story ?

try again ?

worry job no money worry worry

advice ? understand ? help

sorry sad sad

no advice

no job offer :(

get   now   ?

think   social   you

exactly   rules   you   ?

help   you   ?

help   any   ?

big no.

NO   kick   down   plz

bad   ?   forget   OK!

punch   up   ?

always   remember

<3   <3   <3

Rules for Mood-libz for Rules

they say, "rules are rules" say they
here are some rules some are here:

"Sad-lib" = word meaning "grief"
"Glad-lib" = meaning "joy"
"Bad-lib" = meaning "upset"
"Had-lib" = past feeling

Shall we review? Review we shall.

past feeling = Had-lib
upset-meaning = Bad-lib
joy-meaning = Glad-lib
grief-meaning word = Sad-lib

choose Mood-libz for each blank
blank each for Mood-libz choose

Complete it, complete!
You are done are you?

Then congrats - let's play - let's congrats then.

Mood-lib #1

Stone and Stick took a <Glad-lib> walk on a
very <Glad-lib> day.
Stone asked Stick, "How are you?" They said
they felt OK.

"OK is more status than feeling," Stick had
thought,
"Even if it's true, it really doesn't say a lot.
Can you say more about that?" Stick wanted to
connect.
They didn't want to challenge Stone, their stance
was full respect.

Then Stone shrugged and had a look of
<Bad-lib> on their face.
There was such a sense of <Sad-lib> in the
place.
Stone took in a <Sad-lib> breath and held it
rather long.
"I don't know what I'm feeling… everything
feels wrong."

"I can't make myself be <Glad-lib> - so I just
say I'm alright.

I feel that that's about as deep as I can go
tonight.
I don't mean to reject you, but I'd like to be
alone."
Stone said to Stick honestly, while scrolling on
their phone.

Stick felt a little <Bad-lib> and was about to say,
"Fine, leave me alone, Stone!" but they put that
thought away.
They decided not to take offense or indulge their
fear.
Instead, they said, "no worries, I'll get out of
here."

How would you feel if you were Stick? And
what if you were Stone?
How would you treat yourself if you felt so
alone?

connected, broken, connected

you and me and you
we are us are we
they were them were they
as well as
he and she were she and he

it gave language and language gave it
false senses of truth of senses false

there were genders of benders of genders were
there
they made mockery of mockery made they

thieves of certainty of hope of certainty of
thieves
breathe, sit, listen, hear, listen, sit, breathe

now we are confused are we now
oh trickster compassionate trickster oh

erasing experiencing gender experiencing
erasing
brings misunderstanding because
misunderstanding brings
confusion upon confusion

how can we repair we can how
together alone together
now, soon now

to caregivers!

parents, guardians, caregivers
they're are having a hard time out there

maybe you hear them
squawking about behavior
blaming it on spouses
insisting on every privilege
protecting with a hawk's sharp grip

many seek healing for care-given wounds
givers and givens and others

other caregivers–or perhaps the same
are dripping tender loving care honey
without even trying, apparently

from the day you met me
I know you rejoiced
made sure I know I matter
and not just to you

you carried me through
you taught me to reflect
to speak when it matters
to sometimes hold back

I didn't always understand
maybe you always knew
how to find myself
is by letting go of you

to caregivers!

catastrophization of chores

underwear hanging on a kitchen chair
laundry piles everywhere
messy rooms and cluttered closets
enough spare change for bank deposits

dirty shoes and crumpled coats
I think we have too many totes
there's so much trash around this house
I'm not surprised I found a mouse

books and games and art supplies
way too much to organize
and without any help around
I might as well just give up now…

but wait…

just took a little coffee break
now I feel my brain's awake
if I just wait till half past 10
my housemates will be home again

and…

maybe they will help me out?
what's there to get worked up about?

proverbs / tongue-twisters / proverbs

minimal is magical is minimal
magic is minimalism is is magic
magical is motivating is magical

do we use or borrow or gift?
it doesn't stop doesn't it?
gift or borrow or use, we do

ritual practice
halt, cleanse, light
gratitude, squeeze tight
listening, creating
then creating, listening, tight squeeze
gratitude, light, cleanse, halt
practice ritual

applaud, bow, applaud

what's a mid-life crisis?

first of all, what is mid-life? and who do you
think you are?
do you know when I will die? or if I'll get very
far?
is it 40s, 50s, 60s? and is it scientific?
life expectancy's not what it was - it's really not
terrific

some demographic facts and figures from this
day and age
might demonstrate dynamics that make this
question break
did you know lives are shorter here in the USA
than the global average on the earth today?

I can't ignore the fact that if you died at age 9
the middle of your life was literally age 4.5
if a 4 year old child said, "it's all downhill from
here!"
grownups would probably amused and grab
another beer

observing trends over time you'll see we've had
a dip

for COVID funerals, we often couldn't make the
trip
but far more upsetting in this country, by design
white women tend to live to 80; black men to 69

maybe a mid-life crisis has befallen me or you
maybe the world is having a mid-life crisis too
more likely it was long ago, the midpoint of
history
maybe radical acceptance is part of a remedy

there is so much pain and suffering, it calls for
intercession–
weeping, mourning, beating the ground, like it's
my profession
mourning, wailing, wiping snot–it could go on
forever
let's try not to forget that we all got here together

can you hear the profound beats of funeral
processions?
can you hear the mourners crying, full of sorrow,
full of lessons?

to grandparents!

how many grandparents the world over
had grandkids across the planet like you?

hmm?

were you proud? were you sad?
I don't remember when you visited
but I see it in photographs
you look happy to see us!

mhmm!

what if grandparents become celestial beings
watching over the generations and generations?
in the night and day, we'd never be alone
with our thoughts and pains
we could speak them out
divinity would always hear

mm

and we wouldn't have to fear aloneness

mm

grandparents–
you seem like a fairytale
your house is a castle
even if it's a tiny apartment
in assisted living
or a room in a family home
or hospital

you may judge or indulge
maybe tickle and hug

I'm looking for a clue
about why my parents are
the way they are with me
from how they were with you

maybe also how they'll be
with the next generation

hmmm

we're lucky
if we get to know
grandparents as friends

to grandparents!

Generations and Generations

Oma says, "you should…" and "should you…?"
says Oma.
Was Memaw… mom of Mom? Yes, mom of
Mom Memaw was.
Did Grandma's hearing aide impact it? Impact
aide-hearing, Grandma's did.

Y'all had something groovy–something
righteous, something groovy had y'all.

I say language is fire is science is fire is
language, say I.
Words are many-dimensional flames
many-dimensional are words.

Generations changing,
turn and twist meaning,
inspires!
Meaning–twist and turn
changing generations.

Perfect can't exist, can't perfect.
It mustn't all make sense; sense-make all,
mustn't it?

Many younger folks
said "siiick" means "cool" means "siiick" said
folks younger many.

So does "hot" and so does "dope" does so and
"hot" does so.

On slinging singers sing secret stylish slang
songs;
Song's slang stylish secrets sing singers slinging
on.

Parents don't know. No? Don't parents?
Secret code secret, all thanks be thanks all.

Love you all. Carry on. Carry all you love.
You dream to grow, you teach me, help me reach
out.
Reach me, help me teach you. Grow to dream,
you!

thinking about you and you, my friends

we talked about taking a trip together, the 2 of us
but we never decided where or when, so it didn't
happen then

we talked about opening a bed-and-breakfast
serving nothing but toast and custard
of course we'd also serve coffee and tea and
juice and milk
and all kinds of toppings for the toast
butter, cinnamon, mulberry jam...

but you decided to partner up
and do your own version with someone else

you and I, we met at a party
and then I saw you again somewhere
I cried about losing my sense of place
you said my vulnerability showed power
much later, we laughed because
we know it won't matter outside time and space

and you, who wanted to spend endless amounts
of time with me at first

I found it flattering and wanted to spend that
much time with you too
you payed such close attention, pulled me in,
rare earth magnet
emotion so intense, it still scares me to tears

you were there for me when I stumbled hard
on the floor struggling to catch my breath
and you said, "friend, I see you: you're under so
much pressure,"
and, "I go through it sometimes too, it won't be
this way forever."

for what it's worth, I try to be there too, for you
and you and you
we each have our own limits to how much we
can do
I hope we care enough to help each other make
rough edges smooth

speak no truth, no desire

No desire, no truth, no speak

seek wisdom, hope, power
care!
power, hope, wisdom–seek

one another sharing another one
one another sharing meals
sharing another one too

one another sharing feels like friends
and friends like feels, sharing another one too

pursuing pleasure has purpose
has pain!
has purpose, has pleasure pursuing

seek and desire to find
find to desire and seek

Speak no truth, no desire
No desire, no truth, no speak

I am here am I

holding still holding   still   holding still
holding
then yawning   and   yawning then
pain is felt   felt is pain
rarely observed   observed rarely
more often…   unnoticed   …often more

I don't really look   look really, don't
I-
like I can't   can't I
like-
work or try   harder   try or work

still I rest   rest I still
stretched out   out-stretched
hands to chest   chest to hands

meditation begins   so   begins
meditation

singing bowls   chime   bowls singing

breathe in   and out and   in breathe
try not to   think I think   to not try
and   I remain I   and

can you see?   see can you
me placing troubles?   troubles placing me
on floating leaves   leaves
floating on

try and think
think and try
about how systems   hurt   systems, how about
love of money ruins   love   ruins money of
love